T0001332

Invisible Warfare

Liao Yiwu

Invisible Warfare

How Does a Book Defeat an Empire?

The Stuttgart Future Speech

Translated by Michael Martin Day

polity

Originally published in German as *Unsichtbare Kriegsführung*. Copyright © 2023 Klett-Cotta – J. G. Cotta'sche Buchhandlung Nachfolger GmbH, gegr. 1659, Stuttgart

This English edition © Polity Press, 2024

Polity Press
65 Bridge Street
Cambridge CB2 1UR, UK

Polity Press
111 River Street
Hoboken, NJ 07030, USA

All rights reserved. Except for the quotation of short passages for the purpose of criticism and review, no part of this publication may be reproduced, stored in a retrieval system or transmitted, in any form or by any means, electronic, mechanical, photocopying, recording or otherwise, without the prior permission of the publisher.

ISBN-13: 978-1-5095-6294-7 – hardback

A catalogue record for this book is available from the British Library.

Library of Congress Control Number: 2023947422

Typeset in 12.5 on 15pt Adobe Garamond
by Cheshire Typesetting Ltd, Cuddington, Cheshire
Printed and bound in by Great Britain by CPI Group (UK) Ltd, Croydon

The publisher has used its best endeavours to ensure that the URLs for external websites referred to in this book are correct and active at the time of going to press. However, the publisher has no responsibility for the websites and can make no guarantee that a site will remain live or that the content is or will remain appropriate.

Every effort has been made to trace all copyright holders, but if any have been overlooked the publisher will be pleased to include any necessary credits in any subsequent reprint or edition.

For further information on Polity, visit our website:
politybooks.com

If one person engages in a game of chance with an empire, then the forces seem very unevenly stacked, but I won't necessarily lose. As national memory is something abstract and easy to change in accordance with the needs of the regime, the original material evidence that constitutes history can be constantly altered, replaced, and destroyed . . . but the memory of personal disgrace will seep into the blood, instinctively affecting an individual's speech and behavior – and this stigma can never be erased.

Most of my manuscripts are locked up in the filing cabinets of the Ministry of Security, and the agents there study and ponder them repeatedly, more carefully than the creator himself. The guys working this racket have superb memories; a certain chief of the

1

Chengdu Public Security Bureau can still recite the poems I published in an underground magazine in the 1980s. While the literati write nostalgically, hoping to go down in literary history, the real history may be locked in the vaults of the security department.

The above two paragraphs are excerpted from pages 127 and 128 of the traditional Chinese-character version of *June 4: My Testimony*, published by Taiwan Yunchen Culture Company in 2011.[1] Why do I write like this? I've forgotten. Like an old movie of past times and places, each shot is blurred due to damaged film stock. I rack my brains as I replay it, but to no avail – yes, I wrote the draft of that book three times, and the paper later was much better than the paper I used for writing in prison, which was so soft and brittle I had to write very lightly. Paper outside prison has adequate solidity and flexibility, so you don't have to worry about puncturing it with the tip of a pen. Thus, I restrained myself and filled in a page of paper, and then how many thousand? Ten thousand? More? How many ant-sized words can be packed onto a page? Who knows.

I spent four years in prison for two poems, "Massacre"[2] and "Requiem," both of which railed against and condemned the Tiananmen massacre that began in the early hours of June 4, 1989. Fueled by extreme anger, I recited "Massacre" with the assistance of the Canadian Sinologist Michael Martin Day, who was living in my home at the time, and made it into an audiotape, which was distributed to over twenty cities across the country; then, after mustering a mob of sorts, we made "Requiem" into a performance art film. On March 16, 1990, I was arrested and imprisoned. About two dozen underground poets and writers were detained and interrogated, but only eight would be named as defendants in the first indictment in the case against this "counter-revolutionary clique."

I passed through an interrogation center, a detention center, No. 2 Prison, and No. 3 Prison in Sichuan Province. During the two years and two months in the detention center, I wrote and preserved twenty-eight short poems and eight letters, which I hid in the spine of a hard-cover edition of the medieval novel *Romance of the Three Kingdoms*. I used paste to "repair" and restore it before it was eventually taken out of the prison after passing through many hands. In the last prison, No. 3 Prison in northeast Sichuan,

I secretly wrote more than two hundred pages of manuscripts. Over the years, the names and contents of these novel manuscripts have been changed and expanded many times. Now their names are fixed as *The Transmigration of Ants*, *Love in the Time of Mao*, and *Underground Poets in the Time of Deng*. They're all linked to *For a Song and a Hundred Songs*, written after I was released from prison, to form a four-volume book with a collective title of *Go on Living*. The process of smuggling the first three volumes of *Go on Living* out of the prison was extremely complicated. During the sixteen years from January 31, 1994 until September 14, 2010, when I was out of prison and was approved to go abroad for the first time, these prison manuscripts were all hidden in a certain place, thickly camouflaged in all sorts of stuff (such as used diapers). I never thought of doing anything with them, and mentioned them to no one, so I was never really in any danger.

The epilogue of *Underground Poets in the Time of Deng* describes the sudden death of Hu Yaobang, the most enlightened general secretary in the history of the CCP (Chinese Communist Party), in the spring of 1989, which triggered a movement for political reform and spurred millions to take to the streets in demonstrations in dozens of major cities across the country. One of my contemporaries, an avant-garde poet with the pen name Haizi, committed suicide by lying on the rails at Guojiaying Railway Station in Shanhaiguan, a coastal town marking the start of the Great Wall, not too far from Beijing. After that, I was out of prison writing *A Song and a Hundred Songs*.

In the winter of 1992, I was transferred to No. 3 Prison, where many political prisoners related to the June 4 Tiananmen massacre were detained. I slept on a top bunk in a group cell. In the beginning, I wrote some irrelevant random thoughts that I let everyone pass around, but I had secret ulterior motives.

Originally, it was impossible for me to keep these secret manuscripts myself as the cells were subject to random searches. But I knew a paramedic downstairs who had been locked up there since the start of "liberation" in the 1950s. He had been a reporter from the Kuomintang's *Saodangbao* ("Mop-Up Daily"). As he had been detained for so long, the prison guards ignored him. He was well read, and everyone called him

Old Man Yang. Every time I finished writing a fragment, I handed over the manuscript to him to hide.

Old Man Yang knew many prisoners who'd served their sentences and continued to stay in prison for employment purposes. They'd been friends for decades, so he gave them my manuscript to take out of the prison to mail. This went on for a while, but I never expected all the manuscripts would be collected in one place – a very labyrinthine miracle.

When I started writing, I was very bewildered and didn't know what was going to happen, so I used the *Book of Changes* to make a divination, as was my old habit, and the result was "*kun*." The hexagram "*kun*" symbolizes Mother Earth extending in all directions. Could it be that I could write as much as I wanted? Could my pen, like my legs, go all the way to the horizon along the unchanging "*kun*" of the hexagram's six lines? I have been a bit of a talker since I was a child, and suddenly I felt that this Old Man Yang was sent by God.

Our group of June 4 political prisoners was closely monitored from the moment we entered the prison. Of course, someone considered organizing, but it was simply impossible. From my point of view, this prison was a living history museum as several generations of political prisoners were imprisoned there. Our group was actually very lucky. Not only did we receive international attention because of the Tiananmen massacre, but we also had the sympathy of the whole of society then. At the same time, I noticed that there were still many "counter-revolutionaries" there from the 1950s, 1960s, 1970s, and 1980s. These people struggled desperately in the bottomless black hole the Communist Party had created, but they were forgotten, including Old Man Yang, who on the surface supported the government and flattered the prison guards, but in his heart was at odds with the CCP. In order to survive, he had no choice but to remain calm, as if his vocal cords had been severed. At the time I knew him, he was over seventy years old and felt there was nothing to live for, until he unexpectedly discovered that I was secretly writing. Maybe he pinned his slim hopes of seeing history recorded on me, as passing on manuscripts is a very risky thing to do. Old Man Yang had contact with many June 4 political prisoners, and several of them were writing. Why didn't he help others? He disingenuously stated he never had anything to do with such things.

I remember one time when we were chatting casually, he asked, "What do you think about history?"

I replied, "History is like a great tree, and our group of June 4 political prisoners who've received so much international attention is like the part that can be seen from the ground. Absorbing the sun and rain, the branches are flourishing, and the spotlights of the whole world are trained on us. But beneath the ground there are many invisible roots in history. Without roots, there can be no great tree, so if I write history, I will not write the conspicuous part above; I will dig out the roots that spread everywhere in the ground and write of the tears of the roots that will never see the light of day."

On hearing this, Old Man Yang was stunned for a few moments, and then silently walked away. After that, he often came to the cell, I gave him the manuscripts, and there were never any problems. As the prison authorities trusted him, he knew in advance when there would be searches.

Not long after I was released from prison, Old Man Yang and a monk called Sima who taught me how to play the flute were also released. If they were alive now, they would both be over a hundred years old. They couldn't possibly have lived to such an old age. Nevertheless, their spirits deserve comfort in heaven. And I have indeed written about them both in several of my books.

———————————

As my co-conspirator, Michael Martin Day was deported as an imperialist spy. This aroused such sustained attention from the international community that I was released from prison forty-three days early in January 1994, and was sent directly by police car to Fuling, on the Yangzi, upriver from Chongqing, where I was registered as a resident. I'd wrapped a scarf around my head and held a flute in my arms, which gave me the ridiculous appearance of "the returning heroic poet." Unknown to me, the times had changed, and the world was very cold and calculating. I was divorced by my wife in the blink of an eye and was seen to carry a political pestilence that everyone tried to avoid. So, as I couldn't make a living for a while, I temporarily relied on my elderly parents for support.

What surprised me most was the fact that writing outside prison was even more treacherous than writing inside prison, as my manuscripts were confiscated three times! So, the square Chinese characters that I used to make up the manuscripts were even smaller and denser than in the first draft, and in the end, aside from myself, despite my eyesight being severely impaired, almost no one could read them.

According to my records, on page 72 of the traditional Chinese version of *June 4: My Testimony*:

On October 10, 1995, at two in the afternoon, three police cars carrying about a dozen special agents burst in on me. Everything was carried out in accordance with "legal procedures," the officers' ID and search warrant were presented, the entire search process was meticulously videotaped, and all written matter in the house (including manuscripts, letters, and notes) was confiscated. And this included the very nearly completed draft of this testimony – more than 300,000 characters representing my painstaking efforts of the past year and a half.

I was breathing normally, signed with a smile, and asked: "Should I bring clothes?" The answer: "No." I was uneasy leaving my money and valuables at home as I prepared to be the guest of the state for a long time. The agents laughed.

At ten o'clock in the evening, I exited the Baiguolin Police Station in the Xicheng District of Chengdu and was politely told, "Don't leave the city for the next month." Thank God, my head was still on my shoulders and I could still write.

I cursed my carelessness with the foulest language imaginable and set about rewriting with all my might. Without inspiration or passion, the pen slashed the paper to ribbons, and often I could only produce a few hundred words a day. Staring at the paper was useless, and cold sweat couldn't solve my writer's block. But I'd made this bet, I couldn't admit defeat. I wanted to use this to validate my own stupid way of living as an insignificant individual – a bet with the world's largest dictatorship – with writing materials, so that in future my kids won't think their dad was just talking big.

Some details I left out:

Three days before this search, Yang Wei, a June 4 cellmate from No. 3 Prison, visited and brought with him a "June 4 Political Prisoners' Appeal to the United Nations and the US Government" that he had smuggled out at great risk. The four signatories were Lei Fengyun, Pu Yong, Xu Wanping, and Hou Duoshu, who carried sentences of eight to twelve years in prison. I flipped through it quickly and stuffed it into a drawer. Yang Wei said that he had already bought train tickets: "Let's go to Beijing. You go find a buddy as magically powerful as Liu Xiaobo who can pass this letter on to the American embassy." I was hesitating, but Yang Wei grew agitated, tears streaming down his face, and I had no choice but to agree. Among the twenty or so June 4 inmates, Yang Wei was the youngest. When he was arrested late in 1989, he was not yet eighteen. The reason for his arrest was that he had drafted and printed a manifesto "calling on the people to overthrow the murderous regime," posted hundreds of copies everywhere, and signed it as the "China Democratic League" headquartered at No. 1 Times Square, New York, USA. This led to an extraordinarily serious criminal case that rocked the municipal, provincial, and central levels of government. And the police were shocked to learn that the chairman, vice chairman, secretary general, office director, and liaison officer of this wave of "hostile overseas forces" were all one and the same high school student.

Yang Wei and the police have one thing in common, and that is they are in the habit of making silent phone calls. The landline would ring, and I'd pick up the receiver and say "Hello," only to hear the line go dead. Then, a few minutes later, someone would knock on the door. It was the same that time, too, and I thought it was Yang Wei again, but it was the police who came in. We were all caught. After an overnight interrogation, I was placed under "residential surveillance" for twenty days. Of course, the four imprisoned signatories had a miserable time of it, placed in handcuffs and fetters, and confined to cells the size of coffins, denied the sight of daylight for three months.

Then, on the morning of June 6 the following year, the police raided the same cramped apartment again. My parents were at home, hiding in their bedrooms. I was "subpoenaed according to the law" to a nearby police station for twenty-four hours of interrogation. Though the second draft was only a bit over 60,000 words, so the loss was not big, it was still so disappointing! How could I proceed with such writing? I also entrusted people with some works transcribed on official manuscript paper to be forwarded to magazines in Hong Kong, Taiwan, and the United States, but there was no news about them. More than two years after I was released from prison, Deng Xiaoping said that "poverty is not socialism," so everyone was keen to find opportunities to earn money. Except for the top June 4 elites who'd graduated from Beijing's Qincheng Prison, such as Wang Dan, Bao Zunxin, Liu Xiaobo, and a few others, no one was interested in the Tiananmen massacre anymore. People believed the government of butchers was too good to be true. For a provincial political prisoner like me, far away from the political center, the driving force for writing is just the fear of forgetting. Forgotten by relatives and friends, forgotten by everyone, and finally forgotten by myself. Live and remember are the enduring mottos of witnesses from different countries. I wrote poems and went to jail, attempted suicide twice, was humiliated, beaten, electrocuted, and handcuffed countless times, and shared cells with more than twenty condemned prisoners day and night, suffered so much, and overcame so many hurdles (almost like Gou Jian in ancient times, who ate his enemy's shit to survive), but in the end, I was like a piece of shit that is openly shat on a sidewalk, and the value of my existence was in reminding everyone not to step on me. A piece of trash.

That said, it's impossible to return to the womb and be reborn. The good news is that after the searches, my memory and vigilance had been fully tempered. The third draft was written intermittently over a year and a half, and there were also more than sixty pieces of writing outside the prison. The handwriting and density were more compressed than the manuscripts written inside the prison. The final inscription was originally early January 1998, which I crossed out and changed to late December 1997. Then computer shops appeared in major cities in China. I spent a king's ransom of 500 yuan to hire a professional typist to input the official manuscripts, which were sorted out and transcribed into a humming desktop computer. I made several copies of the floppy disk and stored them in multiple places. Afterwards, Hu Jian, an artist friend who worked in a private printing factory, took the initiative to make a scanned copy of the original manuscript, and copied that onto five CDs. However, fortune and disaster can visit at any time, and because Sinologist Marie Holzman published the French translation of *Interviews with the Underclass in China* in Paris on September 23, 2003, French photographer Gao Lei was sent to pay a special visit to me in Chengdu. I couldn't control my vanity, so I made an exception and retrieved the "authentic manuscript" from its hiding place and allowed it to be photographed in my home in Huangzhong Community on the outskirts of the city. So, in this way, word of my book leaked out, and the next day, the special agents of the Public Security Bureau came and confiscated it.

I sit here reminiscing, "in search of lost time," just like Marcel Proust a hundred years ago after he withdrew from Parisian social circles. He finished the seven-volume tome while still young and, later, while idling his days away, died of illness. I shall not pass away like this. What I'm facing up to is the longest-lived communist dictatorship in the world. I fled to the free world so I could continue this game of chance. I've been in exile since 2011, had nine books published by Fischer, as well as a collection of poems, a speech, an audio book, and three other collections by other publishing houses. The latest book is called

Wuhan.[3] When I was writing the first draft two years ago, I was sent to hospital for heart treatment as I'd exhausted myself after working through the night dozens of times. Now that I'm healthy again and sitting here reminiscing, I feel I still have the strength to place that bet.

In February 2002, the original-language version of *For a Song and a Hundred Songs* was published for the first time, in Taiwan, by the Mirror Media Group (Canada, the United States, Hong Kong, Taiwan), founded by He Pin, a naturalized American June 4 exile. The book was titled *Testimony* at the time. Although highly praised by friends of dissident intellectuals such as Liu Xiaobo, Yu Jie, Wang Lixiong, and Hu Ping, it had little impact, selling fewer than two hundred copies. After having the apartment searched and being summoned by the police many times, unable to put up with the harassment any longer, Song Yu, my second wife, filed for divorce. On the eve of my little family's demise, I wrote:

Tomorrow is the Qingming Festival. Before I burn the paper and pray for my sister Feifei's spirit in the sky, I swear that I've not perjured myself. I've

17

treated everything and everyone fairly in my writing, no matter whether the person was good or bad, male or female, I tried my best to restore the truth that I had personally experienced; even though, during this process, due to various flaws in human nature, I was inevitably prejudiced, and just as inevitably applied so-called moral standards.

Moral judgment is necessary in life. In a country without a sense of religion, one must keep a minimum moral bottom line so that one doesn't become a mere beast manipulated by those in power and Mammon. But in writing, moral judgments often become an obstacle to the exploration of human nature. They often replace or distort details with an either–or appropriation of truth. The daily activities of people are not like this, and prison is not like this.

Till today, I'm still used to wearing a smile as a mask to conceal many cruel things. Even if there are tears in my eyes or my heart trembles, I must smile and keep on talking. Blood of the Sichuan Basin flows in my veins, and my nature is moist and gentle, but sometimes I'm disposed to sudden anger, too angry to speak, and I can become prone to violence, bloodthirsty and vicious – my soul full of poison due to long-term persecution. Writing is a slow process for me, a process of detoxification. In a bottomless pitch-black abyss, what is a writer to do? I wanted to escape, I wanted to go crazy. I might lose my freedom at any time, but I wanted to gamble again. I wanted to be in the sunshine, in words, to try to smile calmly, to talk about it. I wanted to live in poverty, but healthily, like a migrant worker who runs around from dawn to dusk. The purpose of tyranny is to turn us into a group of angry lunatics, a group of invalids dominated by our emotions; lunatics and invalids cannot say anything of value about a system or a period of history.

Even if you take my life, I want to strive to be healthy. Even if the police take me away again tomorrow, today I still want to write these words as incriminating evidence, and then go back to my parents' home to accompany my dying father at dinner . . .

Not long after, my father passed away, and our family, following traditional customs, sent his ashes from Chengdu to Lijiaping, a mountainous area in Yanting County, Sichuan Province, hundreds of kilometers distant, where he and I had both been born. All the details about what happened there can be found in the prison manuscript *The Transmigration of Ants*. We invited my grandfather's contemporary, Feng Shui master Luo Tianwang, who was ninety-five years old at the time, to choose the burial place and time for my father, who, at eighty years old, belonged to the "younger generation." I took the opportunity to interview Luo Tianwang several times and induced him to recount the tragedy of the "practitioners of superstition," who, over fifty years ago, when the ruling regime changed, traveled thousands of miles so that at night they could accompany the corpses of those who died abroad in order to allow them to walk back to their hometowns, only to be arrested for doing so. In what seemed like just a moment, a few years later, Huang Wenguang, an American translator whom I'd never met, selected and translated twenty-seven of more than three hundred stories of people at the lowest rungs of society whom I'd searched out for interviews over the course of several years, and had them published by Random House in New York. At the time, May 2008, I was interviewing people among the ruins of the Sichuan earthquake as the stench of decaying corpses hung in the air. It was then that the name "Liao Yiwu" appeared for the first time in the West and attracted a lot of attention. The title of the book of interviews selected by Huang Wenguang, *The Corpse Walker*, is taken from the last recollection of my father's "predecessor," Luo Tianwang, at the time of my father's funeral.

Peter Sillem, an editor at Fischer, who discovered *The Corpse Walker* and bought the copyright for it, asked me for the original manuscript through Huang Wenguang, as the translator he had in mind for the project, Hans Peter Hoffmann, was unwilling to translate from English. At the time, I didn't understand what that meant. Two years later, I arrived in Berlin because of the German translation, published by Fischer, of a similar collection of interviews under the title *Fräulein Hallo und der Bauernkaiser* (*Miss Hello and the Peasant Emperor*).

I applied for a passport to go abroad at least fifteen times; all of the attempts were rejected by the relevant departments. As a last resort, I had to take advantage of local household registration loopholes caused by the Sichuan earthquake to take the risk of acquiring a passport through deception. I then obtained visas from Australia, Vietnam, the United States, and Germany, but was intercepted at customs and my passport was almost confiscated. Fortunately, I have quick eyesight and quick hands, and snatched it back in front of everybody, bellowing, "Murder! Murder!" All the tourists around me were stunned, thinking they'd encountered a madman. I made it onto my plane to Germany, but seven armed policemen seized me just as it was about to take off. Again, those around me were dumbstruck, this time thinking they were in the presence of a hijacking suspect. But a few minutes later, the international media was in an uproar. German Foreign Minister Guido Westerwelle had summoned reporters into his office and issued a public statement: "The German government has tried many times to arrange for Liao Yiwu to make this trip, but, regrettably, we have not succeeded. Germany will continue its dialogue with China, emphasizing freedom of speech and civil rights, and hopes to welcome Liao Yiwu to Germany soon."

Thanks to frequent obstruction by the imperial government, *Miss Hello and the Peasant Emperor* quickly became a bestseller in the German-speaking world, and also landed on the desk of Germany's Chancellor, Angela Merkel.

And this is how the impossible miracle finally came about. At noon on September 14, 2010, Bernhard Bartsch, a Beijing-based reporter for the *Frankfurter Rundschau*, sneaked into my house and immediately asked, "Have you been notified by the police?" I answered yes. He then said: "I'll accompany you. We'll meet at Chengdu Airport later, pretending we don't know each other; and we'll continue that when we transfer at Beijing Airport, and until we get out of customs, when we'll suddenly acknowledge each other." I said okay. Finally, he asked: "Is there anything you want me to take?" I answered yes.

And this was how my prison manuscripts and the scanned copies of original manuscripts recording my time in prison were also able to arrive in Berlin. And so what I'd written eighteen winters earlier in No. 3 Prison, when I'd used the *Book of Changes* divination to get "*kun*," had come true:

坤 *(Kun) Space:* 元亨 *Primary/Origins, Prosperous*
The "Foretelling" states: as to 坤元, all things come into being. Still follow the sky. 坤 is thick and loaded, and virtue is boundless. Containing great splendor, all things miserly or prosperous . . .

䷀ *hexagram: Great Fortune Reaching Heaven*
The "Interpretation" states: The transformational nature of the Earth is revered above all else! Because of you the ten thousand things attain access to the wellspring of eternity. You bring forth life endlessly, yielding to and bearing the boundless changes within the Way of Heaven. The Earth is rich and deep, the ten thousand phenomena move in their cycles; this is such an all-embracing virtue! You are the mother of all mineral resources, the mother of light, the mother of all heavenly phenomena, and all gods. On the vast Earth, the ten thousand things and the ten thousand phenomena all receive their reason for being from you . . .

During my first visit to Germany, Fischer decided to publish my prison autobiography the next year, and Peter Sillem changed the title of the book to *For a Song and a Hundred Songs*; the good news that my old friend Liu Xiaobo had won the Nobel Peace Prize was equally uplifting, too. But I repeatedly declined the frequent requests of supporters such as Wolf Biermann and Herta Müller, winner of the 2009 Nobel Prize in Literature, to remain in Germany, and

I kept my promise to return home as scheduled. The result of this was that I could no longer leave the country. The Chengdu police conveyed the "latest instruction from Beijing," not only strictly prohibiting me from going abroad, but also strictly forbidding me from publishing *For a Song and a Hundred Songs* abroad. If I insisted on going my own way and this resulted in political consequences, I would be sentenced to at least ten years' imprisonment in accordance with the law.

My home was searched, and I was placed under residential surveillance again. Fortunately, I hadn't brought the publishing contract back with me; furthermore, for the sake of my personal safety, Fischer postponed the publication date twice, and finally declared that the book was "indefinitely delayed." I sent a letter expressly stating that I'd rather go to jail again than not have it published, but Fischer remained silent. It's time to end all this, I thought. This convict's war against an empire was too difficult and long. Would I keep at it indefinitely until it consumed me? I was fifty-three years old, and Confucius said, "You know your destiny at fifty," so I felt I had to leave.

I bought four Motorola and Nokia mobile phones at a used goods shop, each of them the size of a goose egg. They were only for communication and sending and receiving text messages. I used them to communicate with an organized crime syndicate on the border between Yunnan and Vietnam, with friends in the United States and Germany, as well as, frequently, with the police, as I vehemently demanded they meet with me to discuss my travel plans. For several months, the police ignored me, and the illegal business between the crime syndicate and me – the equivalent to human smuggling – was concluded for 40,000 yuan.

Before I crossed the border and moved on to Hanoi to fly to Berlin, Vietnamese customs officers extorted my remaining 1,000 euros or so and over 2,000 yuan on the pretext that I had to buy a return ticket. They said that they would return me to the border if I didn't pay. When I landed at Berlin Tegel Airport the next day, I was greeted from afar by the tall figure of Fischer's Peter Sillem, arms open, calling out not my name but "My God!"

That year in Munich, the capital of Bavaria, *For a Song and a Hundred Songs* was awarded the highly respected Scholl Siblings Award by the Bavarian branch of the German Publishers and Booksellers Association. At the book launch, Herta Müller said in her speech:

> A hometown is the place where people are born and live.
>
> Hometowns are places where people are born, live for years, leave, and always leave and return to.
>
> For a man who has survived surveillance, the hometown is the place where he was born, lived for years, fled, and to which he will never be allowed to return. . . .
>
> Dear Yiwu, along with the bitter happiness, pure happiness will also come; in fact, it has already arrived today.

Yes, pure bliss really did arrive. I rebuilt my home in Berlin with a lovely wife and a daughter born into a German-speaking environment. Like *The Gulag Archipelago* and *Doctor Zhivago* and other masterpieces exposing the dark sides of Communist Party dictatorship, *For a Song and a Hundred Songs* also spread like wildfire, with English, French, Italian, Spanish, Swedish, Dutch, Polish, Slovakian, and many other language editions published. However, this war between a book and an empire is still being waged, and the empire will never stop practicing evil unless it is overthrown or dismembered. Throughout the ages, no book has been able to change the darkest parts of history. It's frustrating. I've said many times: both Sima Qian's *Records of the Grand Historian* and Orwell's *1984* are depressing, but when you think about it, a person did actually write *Records of the Grand Historian* and *1984*, so that's not so depressing after all.

Not long after I defected, the police arrested my June 4 cellmate Li Bifeng on suspicion of "funding defection." Later, due to lack of evidence, they turned to fabricating trumped-up economic charges and he was sentenced to ten years in prison. This was his third time in prison – and then, in what seemed the blink of an eye, he was released from prison for the third time after serving his sentence. Over half a year ago, he sent me a letter and passed on some poems through another June 4 prison inmate. Li was now, at fifty-eight, a worn-out old man with gray hair; when we'd met in prison, he was only twenty-seven years old and very full of himself.

He tried to escape from China seven times and was caught on each occasion. Once, after he'd successfully stolen across the border into Burma, he was captured and returned by guerrillas of the Burmese Communist Party and was almost beaten to death by border guards. He is one of the important characters in *For a Song and a Hundred Songs*. If I'd been arrested at the border like him eleven years ago, would I have been able to get out of prison alive? Heaven knows.

An increasing number of political prisoners have not been emerging from prison alive. Among those who have died in prison was four-time convict Liu Xiaobo, the 2010 Nobel Peace Prize winner, who was murdered on July 13, 2017. I racked my brains and repeatedly sought the help of influential friends such as Wolf Biermann, Herta Müller, and Peter Sillem as I tried my best to rescue Liu through the Merkel government, the German Foreign Ministry, and the media of Western countries. But ultimately I failed. Though his widow was released to Germany, the price was too heavy. Moreover, all this was quickly forgotten. China under CCP dictatorship is still the most attractive market in the world for capitalists. New huge deals or huge crimes easily erase any shared memory of Li Bifeng, Liu Xiaobo, and others. In our vulgar and cruel globalized new century, we no longer need these heroes, imprisoned for attempting to move their country towards democracy, no matter whether they are ant-like little people or Nobel Peace Prize winners. I indefatigably record all of this to remind the world, and myself, because I worry that if I succumb to nihilism and lay down my pen, I will have failed absolutely. It is the same as over two thousand years ago when Plato recorded Socrates' philosophical debates, all based entirely on hearsay, while the latter was nearing death in prison. If there had been no words left by Plato, Socrates would also have been erased by time, and his calm attitude towards death would be a mystery that would also have gradually slipped away and would no longer stir people as it does today.

I once proclaimed I "fight for the freedom of others," but I can't seriously recall any prisoner of the empire whose slaughter I've prevented because I wrote of him or her. This truth is suffocating, and I have to stand up, get away from my desk, and go out into the bright sunshine to gulp the fresh air.

We probably never could have imagined that one day the air would be highly toxic. But the era of the Wuhan virus, or of COVID-19, as the World Health Organization called it, would suddenly afflict us all.

Prior to 2019, Emperor Xi Jinping was enforcing the implementation of the "Hong Kong National Security Law," tearing up the international agreement that the old emperor Deng Xiaoping and the British Prime Minister Margaret Thatcher had reached some years before to "not change the social system for fifty years," and dispatched the police force and army, all armed to the teeth, to suppress the protests of millions of citizens. The free port that everyone in China had previously yearned for has become a prison port that everyone is scrambling to escape today, just like Beijing thirty years ago. How time and history have gone backwards! Once again, I recorded and disseminated a long poem, "Second Massacre," and committed the new crime of "inciting subversion of the regime," but have not been arrested and sentenced this time:

Today a gunshot blew out a girl's eye
Tomorrow another blows away a boy's head

The next day Hong Kong blinded, the former Pearl
    of the Orient blind
Rivers of blood flow, corpses everywhere
White-haired parents search, wail, attend funerals
    for children
Like God above seeing stars into graves
The surviving Hong Kongers
Some of them criminals, imprisoned in China
Some slaves, lives worse than dogs'
And still others reduced to orphans of humanity
Scattered in exile all over the globe
Never to return home

Neighboring Taiwan is a transit point for Hong Kongers fleeing to Western countries. I had interviewed many who had been protesters on the streets of Beijing in 1989 and in 2012 published *Bullets and Opium: Real-Life Stories of China after the Tiananmen Square Massacre* in Taiwan and Western countries. I wanted to seize the moment to go to Taiwan to resume my former vocation and write a Hong Kong 2019 version of *Bullets and Opium*.

However, unforeseeable circumstances arose: on the night I submitted a formal application to the Taiwan Representative Office in Berlin – that is, on the morning of January 23, 2020, Beijing time – the imperial government brazenly issued the "Wuhan City Closure Order." All local buses, trains, planes, subways, and boats were suspended, and nearly ten million residents were warned over and over again not to leave the city. By 10:00 a.m. the next day, dozens of other cities in Hubei Province had also been locked down.

All neighborhoods, streets, intersections, bridges, riverbanks, stations, and docks were under military control, and only emergency or hearse vehicles with blaring sirens were allowed to pass. The air was filled with poison, and news of death and related rumors were swamping the Internet. Field army soldiers performing mandatory isolation tasks were all equipped with blue or white seamless protective clothing covering their entire bodies, like strikingly similar automatons from outer space. A privileged few citizens wore special gas masks or anti-virus face shields, while the majority frantically bought food and daily necessities, especially face masks, hours or minutes before the lockdown was imposed until all supermarkets and shops were emptied out. Due to a serious shortage of masks, almost everyone made do with sanitary napkins, paper diapers, grapefruit shells, transparent plastic bottles, and so on, instead.

Something cruelly similar to war broke out.

It was a crime that was worse than the devastation of Hong Kong.

***

Why did this happen? How many people actually died? Where did the bat virus that sparked this war come from? And what about the P4 laboratory over which the military assumed control? The South China Seafood Market that was officially confirmed and then denied as the source of the virus? As the Wuhan P4 laboratory, built with French assistance, is currently one of the world's top virus prisons, was COVID-19's "prison escape" intentional? An accident? The result of management loopholes? There have been no answers to this string of questions that sprang up from Wuhan's citizens at the very start of the outbreak.

Everything will pass, and ultimately no one will raise these questions again. And the long chain of "keywords of the empire" that have emerged, such as "city closure," "zeroing," "masks," "nucleic acid," "testing," "isolation," "health codes," "pop-up windows," "reporting," "monitoring," "warning," "deletion," "control," "detention," "disappearance," and so on, have evolved to become part of the everyday life of the empire's subjects. Why is this happening? Why have 1.4 billion people been reduced to this? Think about how two years ago the people of Wuhan were treated by 1.4 billion people across the country under the personal command of President Xi Jinping, and you will naturally understand why today "we are all people of Wuhan."

Ai Ding, the protagonist of my documentary novel *Wuhan*, flies back to China from Berlin to celebrate the New Year, but can't go home, just because he is from Wuhan; and just because he wanted to know why this was happening, he is repeatedly cursed at, quarantined, and delayed. He is driven away, beaten severely, and finally arrested, whereabouts unknown – purged by his own country like a Jew during World War II in Europe.

In the long poem "My Sole Weapon Is Spit," I wrote:

The on-duty Party leader arrives, looking distraught
The emperor of today has also come, and I say
I don't want to die here

Where do you want to die
At home
You have no home
So die in the city
This city isn't yours, this fatherland
Also not yours
Whose
The people's
I'm not of the people
If you don't have the virus, you're people
If you've got it, you're not. You know
Chernobyl? You can only die here
Like those poor irradiated devils, the dead may only
Lie inside a lead sarcophagus[4]

I couldn't help downloading or copying all I read, saw, and heard that had deeply shocked me. In the beginning, millions, then tens of millions, and finally hundreds of millions of people were forced into home jail. Everyone was overwhelmed by panic and fear, and they all swarmed onto the Internet, scrambling to speak, to post protests, photos, and videos. The number of Internet police in China increased well over twelve-fold, but they were still exhausted and had insufficient time to stem the flood of "prohibited speech" and "reactionary rumors." Nor did they dare go out to arrest people. For about two or three weeks, the imperium's Internet, equipped with the world's most advanced monitoring system, was out of control.

I was swept along, swallowed up by all this, staying up all night for weeks, rescuing and downloading hundreds of thousands of words of materials, until my computer was attacked by hackers and the screen suddenly went black, frozen, and I had to put a sudden stop to my activities. Fortunately, all this first-hand information had also been simultaneously stored on an external hard drive – but my heart, like my computer, suffered an abnormality. I was taken to hospital, and after examination and consultation, it was decided that I should undergo shock therapy, to stop the heartbeat for three to five minutes and then restart it. After the anesthetic was injected, I looked up at the doctor's smiling face and suddenly my mind went blank. When I woke up, I felt only three minutes had passed, but the doctor said it had been three hours.

After being hospitalized for a few days, when I returned home, I reverted to my old ways. My sources of information were mainly the official websites of the Wuhan Institute of Virology and the Chinese Academy of Sciences, domestic mainstream websites, regional websites, Weibo, WeChat, blogs, and so on, as well as citizens' videos on Twitter and YouTube. The content was varied: (1) the past and present of the "Wuhan virus"; (2) how this "bat virus" infected Wuhan, the whole country, and the entire world; (3) hospital overcrowding; (4) crematoriums busy day and night; (5) people from Wuhan and Hubei being arrested across the country; (6) experts fighting amongst themselves about the "source of the virus"; (7) the discussions and name-calling among ordinary people; (8) sudden deaths, suicides, defenestrations, disappearances, homelessness, the blockading of roads . . .

———

Looking back to 2008, when an earthquake with a magnitude of over 8.0 unexpectedly shook the area from Dujiangyan City to Mianyang City in Beichuan County, Sichuan Province, without even thinking about it, I grabbed my backpack and rushed to the epicenter of cracked earth and landslides dozens of kilometers away. I acted out of instinct, more than ten hours faster than the first rescue teams. A year later, my first-hand witness account, *Earthquake Madhouse*, the only one of its kind, was published in Taiwan. I also repeatedly acted as a guide in the disaster area, working and communicating with journalists from the United States, Germany, and Japan stationed in Beijing. But this time when the virus hit, in China as a whole and especially in Wuhan, neither Western journalists nor I could get to the epicenter. If you insisted on going out, what awaited you would be "abnormal isolation" or "disappearance according to law," the legal term for which is "surveillance at a designated residence."

This created an epidemic restriction zone unrivaled in the world in that Western journalists were entirely absent. From Mao Zedong to Xi Jinping, the "primary ruling practice" of the empire has always been: the death toll of any disaster, and likewise the cause of death, is a core secret, and no organization or individual can be allowed to contact, count, or investigate. The "second ruling practice" is to maintain the highest loyalty to the Party and the Emperor, spreading lies by all means, covering up, shifting responsibility, supervision and control, and destruction of a great volume of core confidential files, so that what may lead to a collapse of empire, like that of the Soviet Union, that which constitutes human and materially witnessed "truth," counter-evidence and circumstantial evidence, all vanishes into thin air like smoke. In this way, from top to bottom, disregarding human life, arbitrarily concealing, lying about, and ignoring large-scale deadly disasters becomes the "third ruling practice."

In accordance with the various "ruling practices," the offensive and defensive information war fought by millions of Internet policemen against hundreds of millions of Internet users was bound to intensify. The empire used epidemic prevention as an excuse to deprive the people of all freedom, but while the deadly virus was spreading indiscriminately, there was an explosion of unprecedented freedom of speech. In *Wuhan*, I described the process of this extraordinary rise of free speech through the communication between the novel's characters Ai Ding and Zhuangzi Gui while they were 8,000 kilometers apart. For me, even fiction is built on a solid foundation of nonfiction. Recall how in prison many years ago I said to Old Man Yang, the patron saint of my prison manuscripts, that if there were no unseen roots buried in the ground, there would be no leafy and visible trees of history. This metaphor also applies to *Wuhan*, where fiction and non-fiction coexist. As such, Li Wenliang, an enemy of the state who was once accused by the official state television channel CCTV of being a "rumormonger," will surely become an immortalized hero of truth. Ai Ding, a character in the novel, wrote in his diary:

> Today, the thirty-five-year-old doctor Li Wenliang passed away. A hundred million people were mourning on the Internet. Images of silk flowers, candles like snowflakes and hail swept over every social platform in China. The Internet police and government-hired hands did their best to remove them, but couldn't keep up and ultimately gave up. If Chinese officials had allowed this virtual space to reflect reality, the brigade mourning the "whistle-blower" would have been even more powerful than that mourning Mao Zedong in 1976. The death of old Mao was the death of a remote, godlike figure. Little Li succumbing to the virus himself was a further death blow to those sympathetic hearts who were witnessing the terrible suffering caused by the epidemic.[5]

Then, two citizen reporters appeared one after the other on the empty but heavily guarded streets of Wuhan, like rare animals or fish that had slipped through a net. In the eyes of many people, Chen Qiushi and Fang Bin were also heroes who risked their lives to break the ruling conventions of the empire. Fang Bin, a local laid-off worker in his fifties, rode a dilapidated bicycle as he rushed to a hospital and used his mobile phone to shoot video there. The video was shaky with a voice-over saying: "Eight in the car! Here are eight more dead!!" In front of another live camera, Chen Qiushi cried, "I am not even afraid of death. You think I'm afraid of your Communist Party??"[6] Soon, they both disappeared, but millions of people had watched their live broadcasts on YouTube.

Next came the "intruder" Kcriss, born in 1995 and a former host on CCTV, with a handsome appearance, top-notch protective equipment, professional training, and a German Volkswagen off-road vehicle. Such a fashionable enemy of the state I had not seen before, so I pounced and bit into him like a bloodthirsty shark.

I wanted to use words to build a monument to heroes who search for truth in my book. I would do my best to preserve the lonely cries of Jiang Yanyong, Li Wenliang, Fang Bin, Zhang Zhan, Zhang Wenfang, Chen Qiushi, Kcriss, Ai Fen, Ai Xiaoming, Fang Fang, Xu Zhangrun, Xu Zhiyong, Wang Zang, Wang Liqin, Wu Xiaohua, and other compatriots. I wanted to use the character of Ai Ding as an aggregate of the tragic epic lives of countless independent thinkers. And Kcriss was the first stone of this monument. As described at the beginning of *Wuhan*:

> So now, in an SOS distress video lasting just over thirty seconds, with a car nearly taking flight and white-knuckled hands about to lose control of the steering wheel, Kcriss testifies: "I'm on the road, I'm now being chased by National Security in a car that isn't a police car . . . I'm in Wuhan, I'm driving fast, very fast, they're chasing me, they must want to isolate me . . .[7]

After more than four hours of being hunted, searched for, fleeing, and hiding, Kcriss fell into the net of the law. He had livestreamed his thrilling documentary on YouTube. He had previously gone to a crematorium to investigate the death toll and not had any problems. A week later, he went to the P4 laboratory, the rumored source of the virus, but was blocked by soldiers and had to back up and retreat in his car. And this time, unexpectedly, he had problems. Another who had a similar problem was Zhang Zhan, a female lawyer from Shanghai. Two months after Kcriss was arrested, she went to the same P4 laboratory, but couldn't get in, so she walked along the wall and made a twenty-two-minute video. Her concluding remark is also the conclusion of *Wuhan*: "A restricted area within a restricted area . . ."[8] Over two weeks later, the agents caught her, despite her having no fixed address, and sentenced her to a term in the Shanghai Women's Prison for "picking quarrels and provoking trouble."

Just like Kafka's *The Castle*, nobody can enter, but everyone knows that all the causes of all consequences can be found inside the castle. But how did the Wuhan virus escape through all the various checkpoints? No one knows. And no one can know – the immediate truth will sink into a sea of control by the empire – so the author of *Wuhan* can only record the indirect truth, as Kafka did: those "troublemakers" who, like K, try to approach and enter the interior of the P4 castle will afterwards – all of them – make no more appearances.

English translator Michael Martin Day and I had a heated debate about the DNA of the Wuhan virus. This prompted me to repeatedly examine the research of the "Bat Queen" Shi Zhengli. I learned from the public information on the official website of the Wuhan Institute of Virology that this disaster is a continuation of the 2003 SARS tragedy. The source of SARS was bats, and the intermediate host of the infection that transmitted it to humans was a civet cat in a wildlife farm market in Foshan, Guangdong Province. "In order to prevent a recurrence of the SARS tragedy," researcher Shi Zhengli started there, climbed mountains, and waded through swamps for several years, searching everywhere throughout the nation's twenty-eight provinces and cities before finally discovering an unprecedented "virus reservoir" in a cliff cave deep in the mountains and an old forest in Yunnan. Within this reservoir were dozens of different bat families. So, Shi Zhengli's team started capturing and airlifting a large number of live bats and specimens back to Wuhan, and secretly detained them in a "virus prison" there for various allogeneic cross-species infection experiments. The bat species that allowed Shi Zhengli's team to make a major professional breakthrough was named the "Chinese rufous horseshoe bat" (*Rhinolophus sinicus*), and she also won a scientific award from Hubei Province for this. Swollen with pride, Shi Zhengli stated that her team had finally dredged up the long-sought key from the "virus reservoir." One had to merely insert it into the keyhole and twist gently, and the narrow door of virus infection from bats to humans would quietly open.

"If the virus escaped, nobody could predict the trajectory."[9] In *Wuhan*, Ai Ding, who had been quarantined for many days, climbed over the Internet firewall and read this exclamation and other comments of the British/French microbiologist Professor Simon Wain-Hobson: "The goal of the study of the so-called gain-of-function (GOF) is to add new functions to viral genes so that viruses can directly infect human cells, or enable viruses to spread directly through the air. . . . I think the above-mentioned research by Shi Zhengli's team is totally crazy research, bringing unnecessary risks to humanity."[10]

However, time cannot flow backwards; nothing can be undone. According to the World Health Organization, the Wuhan virus (COVID-19) caused approximately 14.9 million deaths worldwide (ranging from 13.3 million to 16.6 million) in the two years from January 1, 2020 to December 31, 2021, and 84 percent of excess deaths were concentrated in Southeast Asia, Europe, and the Americas. About 68 percent of excess deaths were concentrated in only ten countries, with the United States ranked at the top. Very regrettably, I could not find the death figures for China in this "expert report" published in multiple languages and widely quoted by the media of various countries; and it is even less possible to trace the source of the virus and find causes of death such as those related in the documentary novel *Wuhan*: the scientific research results that Shi Zhengli's team obtained "in order to prevent the recurrence of the SARS tragedy in 2003." I have no intention of challenging the authority of the World Health Organization, but I'm sorry, I have to point out that this "expert report" disregards the countless victims of the Wuhan virus in China and, as such, is an injustice against them.

I must also point out (even if it has been pointed out many times) that on January 23, 2020, when the imperial government officially announced the closure of Wuhan, all customs offices and foreign flights continued operating for several weeks. The key evidence of this that I will provide is the *People's Daily* (see Appendix), which had a circulation of more than ten million copies on the day Wuhan was closed. This is the most authoritative media mouthpiece of the empire, comparable to *Pravda* in Soviet times.

That day the headlines on the front page of the *People's Daily* were as follows:

- Headline 1: Xi Jinping has a phone call with French President Macron.
- Headline 2: Xi Jinping has a phone call with German Chancellor Merkel.
- Headline 3: Xi Jinping and Italian President Mattarella send congratulatory letters to the opening ceremony of the 2020 "China–Italy Year of Culture and Tourism."
- Headline 4: Leading comrades of the Central Committee visit veteran comrades.

- Headline 5: The Wa people sing a new song – Xi Jinping visits a Wa village in Yunnan.

As the *People's Daily* did not mention "closing the city" or the "virus," there can be no doubt it was the decision of the highest authority of the empire to continue to operate customs offices and air flights to the outside world. Hundreds of thousands of tourists from the affected areas flew to all parts of the world as a result.

This is the fate of humanity, as until now, Western countries outside of China have continued to be negligent as regards preventing this severe infectious disease that burst upon the world like a nuclear blast, and remain full of expectations and desires as regards Chinese market opportunities. On January 15, 2020, the first phase of the Sino-US trade negotiation agreement was officially signed and entered into force. President Trump thought that after marathon negotiations led by the White House, the United States had finally won the largest trade war in history, but unexpectedly, eight days later, the tables were turned, and he became the highest-level national leader to have been infected by the Wuhan virus, and ultimately lost his chance at re-election.

German Chancellor Angela Merkel once publicly emphasized that the EU's 5G development should not exclude China, but quickly afterwards her personal doctor was "diagnosed" and she had to self-quarantine for fourteen days; while British Prime Minister Boris Johnson, attending a street rally in person not long after promoting "herd immunity," also tested positive. During isolation, his condition worsened, he had difficulty breathing, and he was immediately transferred to intensive care.

Reminiscent of the eve of World War II, restaurants, bars, and cafés were closed, company employees were not required to go to work, and masks were in short supply. Citizens reminded each other to stock up on daily necessities and stay at home as much as possible. London, New York, Rome, Paris, Berlin, Vienna, Prague . . . hundreds of major cities seemed like Wuhan as tourists disappeared, and they became isolated islands. When 14.9 million people are successively struck down by an invisible "gun"; when the rhythm of life that everyone is accustomed to is suddenly suspended; when human beings have to develop vaccines in a race against virus strains that mutate rapidly; when our descendants also have no choice but to coexist with the offspring of the Wuhan virus (COVID-19) for ever, this reprimand of the rich and powerful virus emperor aimed at Western democracies still rings in my ears: "Some foreigners who've eaten their fill and have nothing to do are trying to dictate our affairs. But, firstly, China does not export revolution; secondly, it does not export hunger and poverty; and, thirdly, it does not torment you. What more can I say."[11] How cruel, shameless, and unscrupulous one must be to be so arrogant. Yes, everything's been turned on its head, what more can I say. In 1991, I started writing in prison. In 2011, I fled China to publish the writings I'd started in prison. As we saw, I used four low-end mobile phones with minimal functions to successfully evade tracking. Who then would have thought that China would become what it is now?

When the "Skynet Project" was bundled with the most commonly used Internet communication platforms in China, it was initially "tested" in a number of defined areas. When this twenty-four-hour monitoring system imported from Western technology companies with huge sums of money was used as an excuse to attack "Xinjiang independence" terrorists accused of attempting to split up the motherland, who would have thought the "Xinjiang experience" of Gulag-style "extended testing" on more than twelve million Uyghurs living in a vast territory of more than 1.6 million square kilometers would eventually cover the whole country? Using epidemic prevention as an excuse, starting from the closure of Wuhan, through the protracted national nucleic acid testing program and the "zero COVID" policy, the "Xinjiang experience" has finally became a law above the law that every Chinese person must obey. Immediately afterwards, Xi Jinping's empire surpassed *1984*, and developed and implemented a "Health Code" system for all citizens. Anyone, taking any means of transportation, going in and out of any place, had to repeatedly scan the "Health Code" installed on their mobile phone. If the "Health Code" showed green, it proved you were an everyday, well-regulated, nucleic-acid-tested, obedient citizen. If it was red or yellow, you were a potential rebel who resisted epidemic prevention, and the police had the right to arrest and isolate you indefinitely. So, when Shanghai and Chengdu were closed in 2022, just as during the closure of Wuhan, all citizen reporters were "dynamically zeroed" – eliminated – like the virus.

However, voices of resistance still emerged. In October 2022, on the eve of the 20th National Congress of the Communist Party of China, in the face of Xi Jinping's upcoming re-election to a third term, like Yuan Shikai in the late Qing Dynasty and early Republic of China, a warrior named Peng Zaizhou, who came from Mao Zedong's hometown, hung the following banner on the Sitong Bridge in the downtown area of Beijing:

> No nucleic acid tests, we want to eat! No closures, we want freedom!
> No lies, we want dignity! No cultural revolutions, we want reform!
> No leaders, we want votes! No to being slaves, we want to be citizens!
> We will strike in schools and at work to remove the dictatorial traitor Xi Jinping!

In any nation, whether it be democratic or dictatorial, it is impossible to "dynamically zero" people's thoughts, dignity, and their lofty spirit in pursuit of truth. "Scholars can be killed but not humiliated" is a solemn teaching of our ancient ancestors that has been handed down to this day. Moreover, it is impossible for the CCP to "dynamically zero" the entire world. It is also impossible to treat the author of *Wuhan* in the same way as the author of "Massacre" over thirty years ago, putting him in prison and implementing "dynamic zeroing" by torture. Even though the CCP has a series of calculations based on wishful thinking about implementing the "communist health code" around the world; even though they occupy a corner of the port of Hamburg in the name of business, I and many other similar freedom-loving Westerners (including those Ukrainians fighting for freedom) have been completely freed from lockdown. To hell with them! I'm not afraid of your cross-border surveillance and death threats, even if I were in China, because my books have been published, from *For a Song and a Hundred Songs* to *Wuhan*. I am waiting for you to try to do something to me, as if waiting for you to publish some exposé about me, leading to an overwhelming readership buying my books.

Evil regimes may seem powerful, but if you look down the thousands of years of history, they don't amount to anything – because their crimes have all been recorded. We feel very insignificant when we create these records, but the testimony we leave behind, in historical terms, will last longer than any evil regime. From this point of view, these regimes are truly not worth mentioning. Over the years, those who have advocated China's rise on the international stage have been short-sighted politicians, businesspeople, and actors who take money without a conscience. But these politicians, businesspeople, and entertainers will also vanish just like that. And human history will be passed down from generation to generation and will be indelible.

In view of this, I am especially grateful to Hans Jürgen Balmes, an editor at Fischer. At first, he accepted *Wuhan* just because of the trust he placed in a writer, and afterwards, we exchanged dozens of letters around the book. I would also like to thank the German translators Hans Peter Hoffmann and Brigitte Höhenrieder, who inspired me deeply with their acute reflections on reading the text, and the accompanying publication report and excellent translation. I would also like to thank the English translator Michael Martin Day. Like the cassette recording of "Massacre" in 1989, we are once again "committing a collaborative crime"; we don't know how many revisions, supplements, and adjustments have been made, so many that the English translation of *Wuhan* seems like a tree, growing and growing until the roots are deep and the branches leafy. We are a model of literary cooperation in the era of the Wuhan virus – although twenty English publishing houses have rejected *Wuhan*, in sharp contrast to its great success in the German- and Chinese-language worlds, yet all these twists and turns are the only road we can take. I think about it, how many years have passed since the release of *For a Song and a Hundred Songs*, and it becomes very clear.

I also know that *Catch-22* was rejected twenty-two times, comparable to *Wuhan*; *Anne Frank's Diary* was rejected fifteen times by English-language publishers after it had been published in Europe; Elie Wiesel, author of a widely publicized memoir, *Night*, about his experience as a Nazi concentration camp survivor, says it's because people are still haunted by the Holocaust. Is it possible that is true? Just as many people go from being unwilling to wear a mask to not being used to taking it off. But I still hope that the editors of the English-language publishing houses that refused to publish *Wuhan* will reread this "COVID-*1984*" and think about whether their past decision was correct.

As I write this, it's the night of November 11, 2022, and I'm sitting in my home in western Berlin recounting this invisible war. My wife and daughter are sleeping soundly. In the night sky outside the window, countless ghosts are smiling. What has passed, what is being experienced, and what is to come are all separated by a pane of glass. A silent uproar. Beautifully sentimental. Time loses its meaning at this moment.

It's time to rest. Time to pour myself a glass of wine. *Wuhan* has been completed, and the promotional work has also been done. In addition to the German and Chinese editions, there are now Japanese and Italian translations. The Italian publisher stated:

This time, Xi Jinping has defeated the whole world, but Wuhan has defeated Xi Jinping. Although he is like Czar Putin, who will not come down once he has gone up, he will die one day, and Wuhan will still be alive and well. This is like the Taiwanese marketing slogan: "A book versus a country."

Unexpectedly, seemingly as soon as the Italian had finished speaking, bad news arrived: on November 24, 2022, the Jixiangyuan community in the center of Urumqi, Xinjiang, had been closed for over a hundred days due to epidemic prevention, and this ultimately led to a fire in a high-rise building from which it was impossible to escape or be rescued. Ten people were officially declared dead and nine seriously injured; but some survivors testified that at least forty people were burned alive. As a result, as with the unjust death of the "whistleblower" Dr. Li Wenliang nearly three years previously, public anger was ignited again, and large-scale police–civilian conflicts broke out in tens of thousands of closed communities in dozens of major cities across China. On the afternoon of November 26, a girl named Li Kangmeng from the Nanjing Communication University held up a blank sheet of paper in front of her chest, silently proclaiming the beginning of the "blank-page revolution."

On November 27, Shanghai citizens arrived from all directions holding blank pages. Breaking through heavy police blockades, they gathered on Urumqi Middle Road to commemorate their dead compatriots. Tens of thousands of people shouted in unison: "Communist Party step down from power! Xi Jinping step down!"

Communist Party step down – history will remember this unprecedented howl. Since 1949, untold millions of people have died tragically due to its tyranny, and this never happened; in June 1989, more than three thousand people died tragically in the Tiananmen massacre, and this did not happen.

——————

The one who led the howl was a twenty-seven-year-old local bartender in Shanghai. He said that he had endured everything for three years, and he'd wanted to cry out for a long time, but he'd been afraid to yell in public, so he just lowered his voice and bellowed: "Xi Jinping!" Unexpectedly, everyone immediately responded: "Step down!" He felt a thrill he'd never felt before as he shouted: "Communist Party!" Everyone immediately responded: "Step down!" And this was repeated several times, like an oil depot alight in a wind, just as the CCP's own "National Anthem" has it: "Each one is forced to let out one last roar . . ."

Many people thought that the tanks would come and that the June 1989 Tiananmen massacre would be repeated, as dictatorships and despots are wont to do. But this time, tanks and martial law troops did not come; instead cities everywhere were "unblocked" overnight! Roadblocks, gates, and isolation fences were dismantled, and tens of millions of anti-epidemic, white-gowned agents employed by the monopoly company running nucleic acid testing suddenly lost their jobs, seemingly because the government owed them back pay. Meanwhile, after the arrest of a few hundred participants, the "blank-page revolution" suddenly fell flat.

With no vaccines and medicines, there were now only people who had just escaped lockdown and the freely mutating Wuhan virus, so the "cross-infection Patriotic Great Leap Forward Political Movement" immediately reached a climax. The number of patients who turned from negative to positive increased to hundreds of thousands, millions, tens of millions, hundreds of millions, and within one and a half months, they exceeded the sum of the number of infected people overseas in the past three years.

———————

On Christmas Eve 2022, news of a death in my hometown in Sichuan Province suddenly arrived from 8,000 kilometers away. My father's younger sister had died of Wuhan pneumonia. She was in her nineties and was the last elder left in his family.

She'd been illiterate and stayed in the countryside all her life. She'd always had a good appetite, ate a lot, accepted everything, and was optimistic by nature. She'd originally shown signs of recovery, but unexpectedly, a few days later, she accidentally fell and broke her ankle. Several of her children rushed to take her dozens of kilometers away to Yanting County Hospital outside the city for treatment. Seeing that she was a long-lived old woman, the attending doctor did what he could. Ignoring the fact that he himself had tested positive for coronavirus, he hung up an antipyretic infusion bottle and was very attentive to her, rolling up her sleeves to check her pulse, and arranging a temporary bed in the corridor outside the clinic.

But the old woman couldn't wait; before the night had passed, she grew short of breath and was gone. Her son said, "I didn't even have time to say goodbye."

In plain sight of everybody, dad's younger sister, who had tested negative, had been infected by a doctor. The hospital expressed its apologies, but not because she'd been infected, rather because the morgue was full, both inside and outside, and when they contacted the crematorium, it was full, too. As usual, the hospital issued a death certificate for her, listing the cause of death as heart failure. Her grandson corrected them, saying, "It's not 'heart failure,' it's 'coronavirus.'" The hospital representative replied: "The Health Commission just announced there were only seven deaths of coronavirus in the whole country, a very small quota, so we can't have any coronavirus deaths in Yanting County."

The family of my dad's sister had no choice but to accept the certificate and rush to the funeral parlor. The dead were like scattered snow, spreading out with no end in sight, but they were all blocked outside a large gateway, and the living were in a lengthy queue at least a kilometer long, lined up to register and make an appointment for cremation. Five hours later, when it was dad's sister's turn, the response from the window was: "You'll have to wait a month." Her grandson said: "We can't wait." The window said: "It's winter, you can wait." Her grandson wanted to argue it, but the window called out: "Next!"

With no place to turn, my dad's sister's family had no choice but to go back to their old home to mourn, lay out her body for a day and a night, and then quietly dig a hole on a mountain in which to bury her.

An unauthorized burial, which was apparently done over ten days ago, is the act of rebels violating the law of the land, subject to fines and imprisonment. But now there are countless new graves on hillsides. In an overseas phone call, someone from my hometown said to me: "The furnace in the crematorium has been burning continuously for several days; people are not as easy to burn as bundles of firewood. To be turned into a handful of ashes, they need to be doused with oil several times . . ."

Hearing this, my head seemed to explode, so I

interrupted: "That's fine, no need for too much detail."

The other party responded: "Well, all in all, our main idea is that there are over ten thousand counties in the country that are as impoverished as Yanting since 'liberation' in 1949 till now. If there's no money to import advanced furnaces from foreign countries that can incinerate more than one or two hundred people a day, it's better to resume burials. There are fewer people in the countryside these days, so once death by coronavirus rushed like a rising tide into the countryside from cities, local governments adapted to local conditions and began bargaining on the fees, and the national economy was immediately revitalized."

I said: "If the Emperor of Steamed Buns[12] heard what you say, he'd immediately 'personally deploy and take personal command.' Moreover, 'Practice cremation and change customs' is like 'Learning from Lei Feng,' also 'personally deployed and commanded' by Great Leader Chairman Mao in the 1950s, and Steamed Buns dare not disobey . . ."

The other party interrupted: "This statement is wrong. From ancient times till now, no matter how great the dead emperor may have been, he cannot hold back a living emperor. Also, enough with the steamed buns please, okay? Just in case my mobile phone number and WeChat account get blocked, and then I won't be able to contact you."

I was surprised and hurriedly said goodbye. Unexpectedly, only a few minutes later, my wife's cell phone rang. She got up sleepily to answer the call. It was from her hometown in Henan Province, 8,000 kilometers away, and her maternal grandfather, who was over eighty years old, had also just died of the Wuhan pneumonia.

Next there was a text message from an old friend from my teenage years, Wang Xiaojing:

> My mother died in Chengdu in the early morning of December 29, 2022. She was ninety-five years old. She passed away on the twelfth day after showing a positive on the nucleic acid test. The Wuhan virus had already entered various systems in her body, and she developed symptoms such as fever, extremely high blood sugar, anuria, low blood oxygen saturation, and low blood pressure. But the doctor didn't mention any of these positive symptoms, and the death certificate only states "lung infection" . . .

Then there was a series of pictures on the Internet illustrating that funeral homes all over the country were in a state of emergency, and that there was an urgent need for corpse trucks, paper coffins, and body bags. In a residential community in a prosperous area of Shanghai, thick smoke billowed, and people burned bodies in the open air. In a video on her mobile phone, a woman said:

> The most terrifying thing is not that people die every day, but that a large number of corpses are still in people's homes. They're there from one to seven days, both in Shanghai and across the country. All the crematoriums have instituted a lottery system, and we all line up at 4:30 in the morning to get into it. If you're unlucky and can't get a number, you have to go early again the next day. . . . See this friend, he died the day before yesterday and his corpse has been laid out at home for three days. It all scares me to death.

I was scared to death, too. Dylan Thomas's "Elegy" instantly came to mind: "Noon, and night, and light. The rivers of the dead."

———

This is a river flowing in China that cannot be counted, cannot be questioned, has neither name nor surname, and neither beginning nor end. The moment Wuhan was locked down in 2020, as I wrote my documentary novel based on the events, I began to trace the source of this virus (COVID-*1984*) that has dominated and raped human history, and that source was the South China Seafood Market in Wuhan, or was it the P4 laboratory of the Wuhan Institute of Virology? Time has streamed on, but the scientific community in the East and the West cannot answer this very modest question.

The ensuing question is: why did China's customs offices and international flights have to remain open when Wuhan was locked down, allowing the virus to go global and causing excess deaths outside of China? Why do we have to repeat the old trick again now, opening the country for a second time, letting the Wuhan virus, which has multiplied and mutated for countless generations, go global once more through virus-positive tourists who've climbed out over piles of corpses?

I seem to hear the Communist Party Central Committee headed by Xi Jinping saying to the

1.4 billion Chinese people: "You don't want to sit jailed at home, you don't want COVID-*1984*, you want to launch a 'blank-page revolution,' you want us to step down? Well then, get out of your homes immediately and taste the 'freedom' we have given you – immediately released from dynamic zeroing. Aside from everybody being positive, there is no excess of anything: medicine, food, assistance, jobs, resources – there is no surplus; even after death, there is no excess of morgues and crematoria. There is surplus abroad, where democracy and human rights are emphasized, so you can pay for it yourselves, virus carriers who don't want to be slaves. Surge out into the outside world like a massive wave – herd immunity or perish! Like the lyrics of 'The Internationale': 'Each at the forge must do their duty/ And we'll strike while the iron is hot!'"

––––––––––

But they will not succeed. This empire, which must be fragmented, will not succeed. Neither Putin nor Xi Jinping will succeed. Just as Lenin, Hitler, Stalin, Mao Zedong, and Deng Xiaoping could not succeed. Yes, in the catastrophes, one after another, caused by the virus of dictatorship, countless innocent people die tragically, but our records in words and images of the dictatorship's evil will let them live on.

Let the nameless dead, whose sky is as vast as the earth, live for ever as witnesses to evil.

November 11, 2022, at Schloss Charlottenburg
November 16, 2022, revision
November 27, 2022, revision
December 31, 2022–January 6, 2023, final revision

Appendix

The *People's Daily* on the day Wuhan was closed.

Notes

1 Published in English in 2013 by New Harvest, in a translation by Huang Wenguang, as *For a Song and a Hundred Songs: A Poet's Journey through a Chinese Prison*.
2 This poem was also published in English with the alternate title "Slaughter."
3 *Wuhan: A Documentary Novel*, trans. Michael Martin Day, Cambridge: Polity, 2024.
4 This poem is reproduced in full in *Wuhan*, pp. 233–245 (quote at p. 242).
5 *Wuhan*, p. 71.
6 *Wuhan*, p. 17.
7 *Wuhan*, p. 7.
8 *Wuhan*, p. 224.
9 *Wuhan*, p. 152.
10 *Wuhan*, p. 144.
11 Speech by Xi Jinping on a state visit to Mexico, February 11, 2009, https://www.youtube.com/watch?v=uZv0B28Gx-c.

12 A satirical nickname for Xi Jinping, meaning he's useless for most things but good at eating steamed buns at least.